More Women in Science Coloring and Activity Book

For Women in Engineering, Women in Medicine, and Women in Botany

Illustrated by Danielle Pioli

Science Wide Open series written by Mary Wissinger

Science, Naturally!
An imprint of Platypus Media, LLC
Washington, D.C.

T0020247

More Women in Science Coloring and Activity Book:
For Women in Engineering, Women in Medicine, and Women in Botany
Paperback first edition • September 2022 • ISBN: 978-1-938492-87-7

Illustrated by Danielle Pioli
Science Wide Open series written by Mary Wissinger
Original series concept by John J. Coveyou

Cover Design: Caitlin Burnham, Washington, D.C.
Book Design: Marlee Brooks, Chevy Chase, MD
Editors:
    Marlee Brooks, Chevy Chase, MD
    Caitlin Burnham, Washington, D.C.
    Hannah Thelen, Silver Spring, MD

Enjoy all the titles in the Science Wide Open series
    Women in Biology • Las mujeres en la biología
    Women in Chemistry • Las mujeres en la química
    Women in Physics • Las mujeres en la física
    Women in Engineering • Las mujeres en la ingeniería
    Women in Medicine • Las mujeres en la medicina
    Women in Botany • Las mujeres en la botánica
    Women in Science Coloring and Activity Book
    More Women in Science Coloring and Activity Book

Published by:
    Science, Naturally! – An imprint of Platypus Media, LLC
    750 First Street NE, Suite 700
    Washington, DC 20002
    202-465-4798 • Pax: 202-558-2132
    Info@ScienceNaturally.com • ScienceNaturally.com

Distributed to the book trade by:
    National Book Network (North America)
        301-459-3366 • Toll-free: 800-462-6420
        CustomerCare@NBNbooks.com • NBNbooks.com
    NBN International (worldwide)
        NBNi.Cservs@IngramContent.com • Distribution.NBNi.co.uk

10 9 8 7 6 5 4 3 2 1

Printed in the United States.

Design your own bridge!
What is it made of? How long will it be? How does it stay up?

Ynés Mexía

Dr. Janaki Ammal

Can you use your observation skills to find
the seven differences between these pictures?

Dr. Treena Livingston Arinzeh

X-Ray Image

Heart

Test Tubes

Sickle Cell

Protractor

Can you list four things that you should keep in a first aid kit?

1. _____

2. _____

3. _____

4. _____

Dr. Helen Taussig

Huang Daopo

Elizabeth Coleman

Hedy Lamarr

Can you think of an invention that would help solve a problem or make people's lives easier? Write or draw your idea below and brainstorm what you would need to build it!

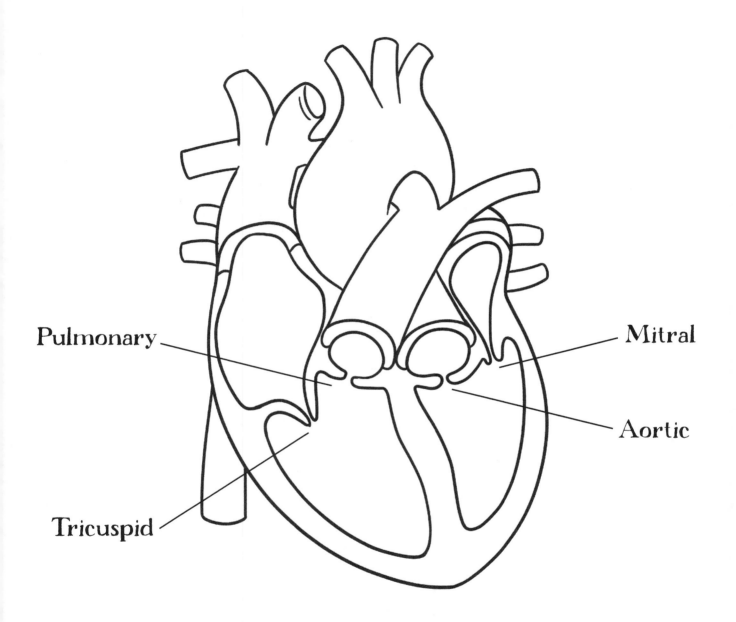

Pulmonary

Mitral

Aortic

Tricuspid

Dr. Angella Ferguson

Fill up the jars!

Xoquahtli

There are many different kinds of jobs that help people take care of their health. Which one would you want to be? Can you think of any more that aren't on this list?

PHYSICIAN: Diagnoses and treats patients. There are many specialists that focus on different things, such as cardiologists (heart doctors), and ophthalmologists (eye doctors).

REGISTERED NURSE: Works directly with patients to help treat and care for them.

PHARMACIST: Provides medications to patients and medical facilities.

NURSE MIDWIFE: Specializes in women's health, pregnancy, and childbirth.

SURGEON: Performs operations and other medical procedures on patients.

PHYSICAL THERAPIST: Helps patients recover from injuries using stretching, exercise, massage, and special equipment.

ANESTHESIOLOGIST: Gives patients a careful combination of medications to put them in a sleep-like state for surgery.

PARAMEDIC: Specializes in emergency medical care, usually working in an ambulance.

HOME HEALTH AIDE: Meets patients in their homes to provide care for them.

PHLEBOTOMIST: Specializes in drawing blood, usually for testing or donations.

PSYCHIATRIST: Diagnoses and treats mental illness through therapy and medication.

RADIOLOGIST: Uses medical imaging, such as CT, MRI, and PET scans, X-rays, and ultrasounds, to see inside the body.

Dr. Wangari Maathai

Tu Youyou

Unscramble the words!

SAQUHS   NEBAS   NOCR   NFSOWRLEU

_____   _____   _____   _____

DAGRNE   TANPL   WOGR   TOYBAN

_____   _____   _____   _____

Peseshet

Design your own original cure all!
What would you put in it to make people feel better?

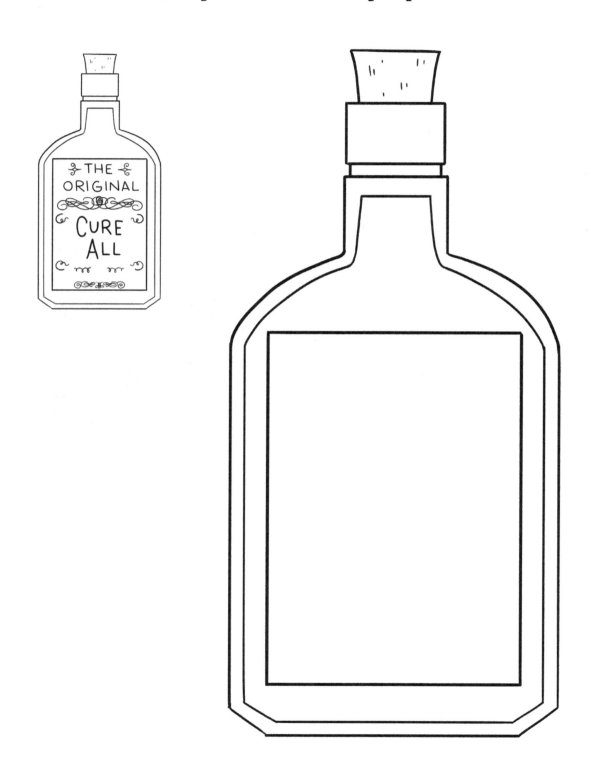

Mary the Prophetess

Waheenee / Buffalo Bird Woman

Sandra Cauffman

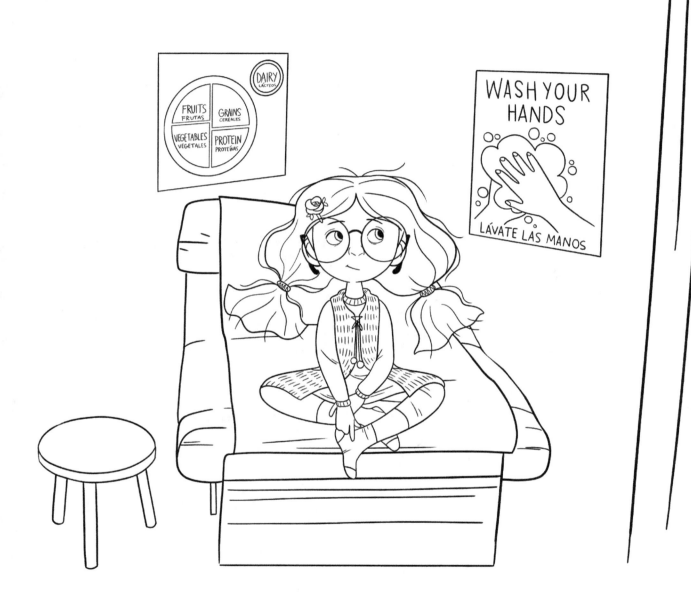

Doctors in the past used things like plants and honey to make medicines. Draw yourself as a doctor with all the ingredients you would use for your own special medicine.

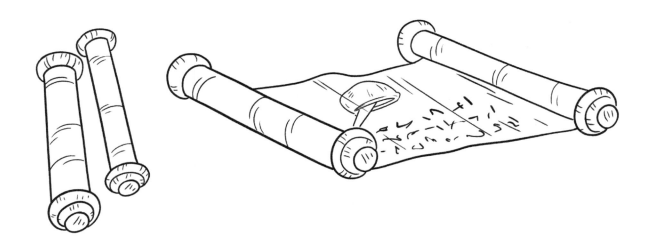

Can you match the scientists to their amazing creations?
The first one is done for you.

Scientist:	Created:
Huang Daopo	A cure for malaria
Dr. Angella Ferguson	The Green Belt Movement
Dr. Wangari Maathai	A more efficient cotton spinning wheel
Hedy Lamarr	The Brooklyn Bridge
Tu Youyou	A way to test for sickle cell disease
Dr. Janaki Ammal	A sweeter type of sugarcane
Emily Warren Roebling	A frequency hopping device for radio waves

Dr. Gerty Cori

Discover the entire Science Wide Open series!

Hardback: $14.99 • Paperback: $12.95 • eBook: $11.99
8 x 8" • 40 pages • Ages 7-10

Book 1
Women in Biology

Hardback: 978-1-945779-09-1
Paperback: 978-1-938492-30-3
Spanish: 978-1-938492-07-5

Book 2
Women in Chemistry

Hardback: 978-1-945779-10-7
Paperback: 978-1-938492-31-0
Spanish: 978-1-938492-32-7

Book 3
Women in Physics

Hardback: 978-1-945779-11-4
Paperback: 978-1-938492-34-1
Spanish: 978-1-938492-35-8

Book 4
Women in Engineering

Hardback: 978-1-938492-52-5
Paperback: 978-1-938492-53-2
Spanish: 978-1-938492-95-2

Book 5
Women in Medicine

Hardback: 978-1-938492-55-6
Paperback: 978-1-938492-56-3
Spanish: 978-1-938492-96-9

Book 6
Women in Botany

Hardback: 978-1-938492-58-7
Paperback: 978-1-938492-59-4
Spanish: 978-1-938492-97-6

Women in Science
Coloring and Activity Book

A companion to books 1–3
ISBN: 978-1-938492-86-0

More Women in Science
Coloring and Activity Book

A companion to books 4–6
ISBN: 978-1-938492-87-7

Science, Naturally!
ScienceNaturally.com
Info@ScienceNaturally.com

 Sparking curiosity through reading